asymmetrical quilts

LEISURE ARTS, INC.
Little Rock, Arkansas

Table of Contents

Production

Graphic Art - Phyllis Dobbs
Photography - Becky Stayner - Sunnyhousestudio.com
Photostyling - Phyllis Dobbs
Quilting - Lisa Mullins - Wanderingstitches.com

EDITORIAL STAFF
Vice President Editorial: Susan White Sullivan
Quilt and Craft Publications Director: Cheryl Johnson
Special Projects Director: Susan Frantz Wiles
Senior Prepress Director: Mark Hawkins
Art Publications Director: Rhonda Shelby
Imaging Technician: Stephanie Johnson
Prepress Technician: Janie Marie Wright
Publishing Systems Administrator: Becky Riddle
Mac Information Technology Specialist: Robert Young

BUSINESS STAFF
President and Chief Executive Officer: Rick Barton
Vice President of Sales: Mike Behar
Director of Finance and Administration: Laticia Mull Dittrich
National Sales Director: Martha Adams
Creative Services: Chaska Lucas
Information Technology Director: Hermine Linz
Controller: Francis Caple
Vice President, Operations: Jim Dittrich
Retail Customer Service Manager: Stan Raynor
Print Production Manager: Fred F. Pruss

Library of Congress Control Number: 2011934168

ISBN-13: 978-1-60900-373-9

Asymmetrical Quilts

Go off center and enjoy the fun of creating unique quilts with asymmetrical designs. These 9 throw and wall hanging sized quilts will add dramatic designs to your decor. Traditional blocks are combined in very non-traditional arrangements. Whimsical appliqué adorns some of the quilts for exciting floral designs. The designs are created for all skill levels from beginning to advanced, so there is something for everyone in *Asymmetrical Quilts*.

Phyllis Dobbs was enticed into designing quilts by a love of fabric and design, combined with a family history of quilt making. Surrounded by stacks of quilts sewn by her great-grandmothers, grandmother and aunt, she is constantly inspired by tradition but loves to put fun and unexpected twists into her designs. After years of designing quilts for books and magazines, Phyllis turned her artistic talents into designing fabrics that, along with her quilt designs, are influenced by her sense of whimsy and love of vibrant colors. Her art is also licensed for gift, home decor and garden products. A graduate of the University of Alabama, Phyllis lives in Birmingham, AL with her husband and cat.

To see more of Phyllis' designs, please visit her blog at Phyllisdobbs.info and her web site at Phyllisdobbs.com.

FINISHED QUILT SIZE - 52" x 61$^{1}/_{2}$" (132 cm x 156 cm)
FINISHED BLOCK SIZE - 9$^{1}/_{2}$" x 9$^{1}/_{2}$" (24 cm x 24 cm)

Fabric requirements:

The yardage requirement is based on 43" to 44" (109/112 cm) wide fabric.

- 1$^{3}/_{4}$ yds (1.60 m) - multicolor turquoise large print fabric
- 1$^{1}/_{4}$ yds (1.14 m) - turquoise floral print fabric
- $^{3}/_{8}$ yd (34 cm) - dark multicolor turquoise small print fabric
- $^{1}/_{4}$ yd (23 cm) - light multicolor turquoise small print fabric
- $^{1}/_{4}$ yd (23 cm) - turquoise solid tonal fabric
- $^{1}/_{2}$ yd (46 cm) - stripe fabric
- $^{5}/_{8}$ yd (57 cm) - green print fabric
- $^{1}/_{2}$ yd (46 cm) - fabric for binding
- 3$^{1}/_{2}$ yds (3.20 m) - fabric for backing

You will also need:
60" x 70" (155 cm x 178 cm) piece of batting
Coordinating thread for quilting

Cutting the pieces:

Follow Rotary Cutting instructions on page 61 to cut the fabric. Cut pieces from selvage to selvage. The measurements include $^{1}/_{4}$" seam allowance. The borders are cut longer than necessary. Trim after sewing.

From the multicolor turquoise large print:
Cut left side border 65" x 4$^{1}/_{2}$" (This will require piecing for 65").
Cut bottom border 56" x 4$^{1}/_{2}$" (This will require piecing for 56").
Cut 14 strips 10$^{3}/_{8}$" x 2$^{7}/_{8}$".
Cut 14 strips 8" x 2$^{7}/_{8}$".
Cut 24 strips 2$^{1}/_{2}$" x 7$^{7}/_{8}$".

From the turquoise floral print fabric:
Cut right side border 65" x 4$^{1}/_{2}$" (This will require piecing for 65").
Cut top border 56" x 4$^{1}/_{2}$" (This will require piecing for 56").
Cut 10 strips 10$^{3}/_{8}$" x 2$^{7}/_{8}$".
Cut 10 strips 8" x 2$^{7}/_{8}$".

(Cutting continued on page 6)

Imagination

From the dark multicolor turquoise small print:
Cut 7 blocks $5^{5}/_{8}$" square. Cut blocks in half diagonally to form 14 half square triangles (HST's).
Cut 6 blocks $3^{1}/_{4}$" square.

From the light multicolor turquoise small print:
Cut 2 blocks $5^{5}/_{8}$" square. Cut blocks in half diagonally to form 4 HST's.

From the turquoise solid tonal fabric:
Cut 4 strips $10^{3}/_{8}$" x $2^{7}/_{8}$".
Cut 4 strips 8" x $2^{7}/_{8}$".

From the stripe fabric:
Cut 2 side border pieces 50" x $3^{1}/_{2}$" (This will require piecing for 50").
Cut 2 top/bottom border pieces 41" x $3^{1}/_{2}$".

From the green print fabric:
Cut 5 blocks $5^{5}/_{8}$" square. Cut blocks in half diagonally to form 10 HST's.
Cut 12 pieces $7^{1}/_{4}$" x $2^{1}/_{2}$".
Cut 4 border corner blocks $3^{1}/_{2}$" square.
Cut 12 pieces $3^{1}/_{4}$" x $2^{1}/_{2}$".
Cut 12 blocks $2^{3}/_{4}$" square. Cut blocks in half diagonally to form 24 HST's.

For the binding:
Cut 6 strips $2^{1}/_{2}$" x width of fabric.

Assembling the quilt top:

Sew all pieces right sides together and sew with a $^{1}/_{4}$" seam allowance. Press all seams as you sew, pressing the seams toward the darker fabric.

1. **Instructions for sewing the center pieces for blocks 1 and 2:** Sew the 8" x $2^{7}/_{8}$" strips to the left edge of a HST, aligning bottom edges. Sew the $10^{3}/_{8}$" x $2^{7}/_{8}$" strips to the bottom edges. Trim the edges of the strips even as shown in Fig. 1.

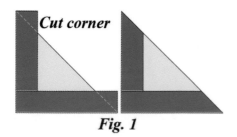

Fig. 1

2. **Block 1.** Sew the 8" and $10^{3}/_{8}$" turquoise floral print strips to the $5^{5}/_{8}$" green print HST's as instructed in number 1 above. Make 10. Sew the 8" and $10^{3}/_{8}$" multicolor turquoise large print strips to the $5^{5}/_{8}$" dark multicolor turquoise small print HST's. Make 10 (Fig. 2)

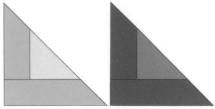

Fig. 2   Sew 10 of each

3. Sew 1 of each triangle unit together on the diagonal edges. Make 10.

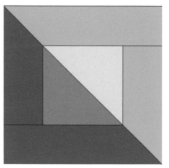

Fig 3   Make 10 Blocks

4. **Block 2.** Sew the 8" and $10^{3}/_{8}$" turquoise floral print strips to the $5^{5}/_{8}$"green print HST's as instructed in number 1 above. Make 4. Sew the 8" and $10^{3}/_{8}$" turquoise solid tonal strips to the $5^{5}/_{8}$" light multicolor turquoise small print HST's. Make 4 (Fig. 4).

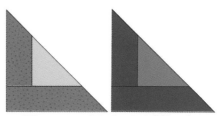

Fig. 4   Make 4 of Each

7

5. Sew 1 of each triangle unit together on the diagonal edges. Make 4 blocks.

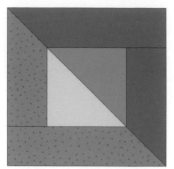

Fig. 5   *Make 4 Blocks*

6. **Block 3.** Sew the 3¼" x 2½" green print pieces to top and bottom edges of the 3¼" square dark multicolor turquoise print. Sew the 7¼" x 2½" green print pieces to the side edges.

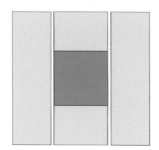

Fig. 6   *Make 6*

7. Cut both ends of the 7⅞" x 2½" multicolor large print pieces at a 45° angle as shown in Fig. 7. Sew a piece to each side edge of the block created in number 6 above, sewing to two opposite side edges, then the remaining 2 edges.

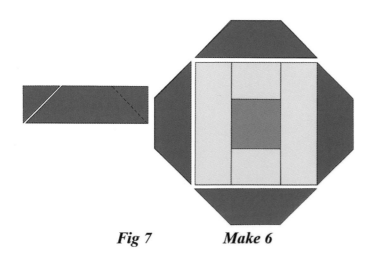

Fig 7   *Make 6*

8. Sew a 2¾" green print HST to each of the 4 edges (Fig. 9). Make 6.

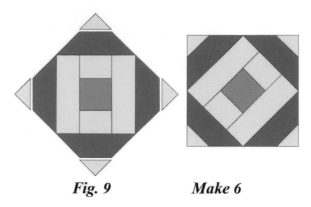

Fig. 9   *Make 6*

9. Sew 4 blocks together to make a row. Make 5 rows. Arrange the blocks for each row as shown in Fig. 10. Arrange the rows as shown and sew rows together.

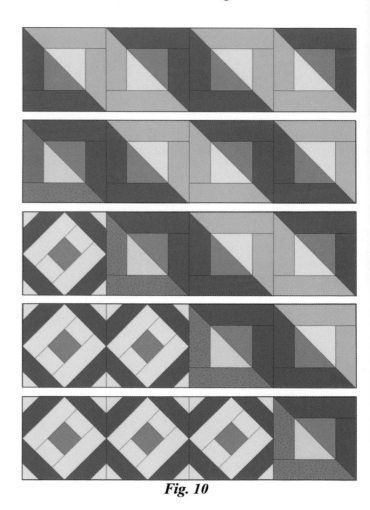

Fig. 10

10. Sew a 50" long stripe border piece to each side edge. Trim any excess border length allowing for a ¼" seam allowance.

11. Pin the 41" stripe border pieces to the top and bottom edges. Trim excess ends off allowing for

a ¼" seam allowance. Sew corner blocks to each end of the top and bottom border pieces, matching seams with the side borders. Sew borders.

12. Following the instructions on page 62 for mitering the border corners, sew the turquoise floral print border pieces to the top and right side edges. Sew the multicolor turquoise large print border pieces to the bottom and left side edges.

Completing the quilt:

Follow the quilting instructions on page 62 to layer and quilt as desired. Our quilt was machine long arm quilted.

Follow the binding instructions on page 63 to attach the binding.

FINISHED QUILT SIZE - 44¹/₂" x 59¹/₄" (108 cm x 151 cm)

Fabric requirements:

The yardage requirement is based on 43" to 44" (109/112 cm) wide fabric.

- ³/₈ yd (24 cm) - dark green print fabric
- ¹/₂ yd (46 cm) - pink leopard skin print fabric
- ⁵/₈ yd (57 cm) - dark pink small print fabric
- ¹/₂ yd (46 cm) - wine print fabric
- ¹/₂ yd (46 cm) - green leopard skin print fabric
- ⁷/₈ yd (80 cm) - green/beige print fabric
- ⁷/₈ yd (80 cm) - bright pink print fabric
- ¹/₂ yd (46 cm) - tan print fabric
- ¹/₈ yd (12 cm) - green zebra print fabric
- ¹/₂ yd (46 cm) - red zebra print fabric
- ¹/₄ yd (23 cm) - blue print fabric
- ¹/₂ yd (46 cm) - fabric for binding
- 3 yards (2.74 m) - fabric for backing

You will also need:
53" x 67" (135 cm x 170 cm) piece of batting
Coordinating thread for quilting

Windmills of Color

Cutting the pieces:

Follow Rotary Cutting instructions on page 61 to cut the fabric. Cut pieces from selvage to selvage. The measurements include ¼" seam allowance. The borders and long strip pieces are cut longer than necessary. Trim after sewing.

From the dark green print fabric:
Cut 2 pieces $3^5/8$" x 28".
Cut 4 blocks $4^3/4$" square. Cut the blocks diagonally for 8 half square triangles (HST's).

From the pink leopard skin print fabric:
Cut 1 block $14^1/4$" square. Cut the block diagonally twice for 4 quarter square triangles (QST's).

From the dark pink small print fabric:
Cut 2 side border pieces 3" x 57" (cut and piece for 57").
Cut 2 top/bottom border pieces 3" x 42".
Cut 2 blocks $7^3/8$" square. Cut the blocks diagonally for 4 HST's.

From the wine print fabric:
Cut 1 block $8^5/8$" square. Cut the block diagonally for 2 HST's.
Cut 4 blocks $5^1/8$" square.
Cut 4 border corner blocks $2^3/4$" square.

From the green leopard skin print fabric:
Cut 2 border pieces $3^1/2$" x 38".
Cut 2 blocks $4^3/4$" square. Cut the blocks diagonally for 4 HST's.
Cut 4 border corner blocks 3" square.

From the green/beige print fabric:
Cut 1 block $14^1/4$" square. Cut the block diagonally twice for 4 quarter square triangles (QST's).
Cut 4 blocks $5^7/8$" square. Cut the blocks diagonally for 8 HST's (You will need to use only 7).

From the bright pink print fabric:
Cut 1 block $14^1/4$" square. Cut the block diagonally twice for 4 quarter square triangles (QST's).

Cut 1 block $8^5/8$" square. Cut the block diagonally for 2 HST's.
Cut 4 blocks $5^7/8$" square. Cut the blocks diagonally for 8 HST's (You will need to use only 7).

From the tan print fabric:
Cut 2 blocks $7^3/4$" square. Cut the block diagonally twice for 8 quarter square triangles (QST's). (You will need to use only 6.)
Cut 2 blocks $7^3/8$" square. Cut the blocks diagonally for 4 HST's.
Cut 2 blocks $4^1/8$" square. Cut the blocks diagonally for 4 HST's.

From the green zebra print fabric:
Cut 1 piece $42^1/4$" x $1^3/4$".

From the red zebra print fabric:
Cut 2 side border pieces $2^3/4$" x 53" (Cut and piece strips for 53").
Cut 2 top/bottom border pieces $2^3/4$" x 37".

From the blue print fabric:
Cut 6 blocks $4^3/4$" square. Cut the blocks diagonally for 12 HST's.

For the binding:
Cut 5 strips $2^1/2$" x width of fabric.

Assembling the quilt top:

Sew all pieces right sides together and sew with a ¼" seam allowance. Press all seams as you sew, pressing the seams toward the darker fabric.

1. **Block 1**. Sew a $7^3/8$" dark pink small print HST and a $7^3/8$" tan print HST together. Make 4 (Fig. 1, A). Sew 2 blocks together arranged as shown in Fig. 1, B. Make 2 units. Sew the 2 two-block units together. Make 1.

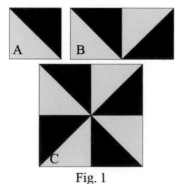

Fig. 1

13

2. Sew a 14¼" bright print QST to the top and bottom edges. Sew the remaining 2 QST's to the side edges.

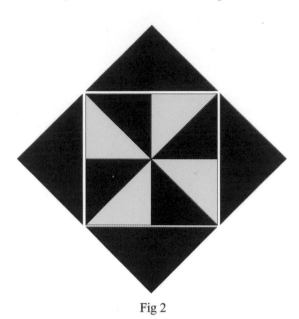

Fig 2

3. Sew a 14¼" pink leopard skin QST to a 14¼" green/beige QST. Make 4 (Fig. 3, A). Sew a QST unit to 2 opposite side edges of the main block. Sew 2 QST units to the remaining 2 edges of the block (Fig. 3).

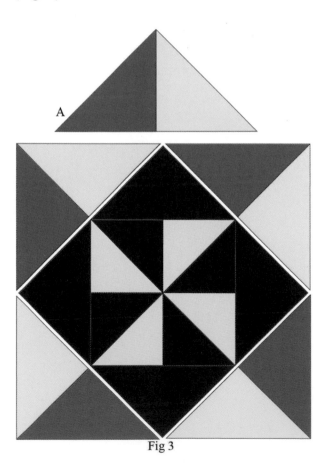

Fig 3

4. Sew a 3⅝" x 28" dark green piece to the top and bottom edges. Trim ends. See Fig. 10, A for the arrangement.

5. **Block 2.** Sew the 7¾" tan print QST's to the 5⅛" wine print blocks. Sew in units arranged as shown in the Fig. 4 below, sewing a tan piece to 2 opposite side edges of the blocks. Sew the units together. Sew the 4⅛" tan print HST's to the corner ends of the row, as shown. Make 1 row.

Fig. 4

6. Sew the unit in number 5 above to the bottom edge of the main block unit, sewing to the bottom edge of the dark green strip. See Fig. 10, A for the arrangement.

7. **Block 3.** Sew a 4¾" blue HST to a 4¾" green leopard skin print HST. Make 4. Sew 2 blocks together as arranged in Fig. 5. Make 2. Sew 2 two-block units together. Make 1 block.

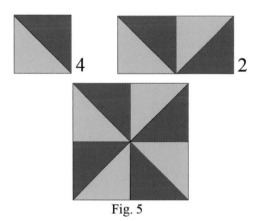

Fig. 5

8. Sew a 4¾" blue HST to a 4¾" dark green print HST. Make 8. Sew 2 blocks together as arranged in Fig. 6. Make 4. Sew 2 two-block units together. Make 2 blocks.

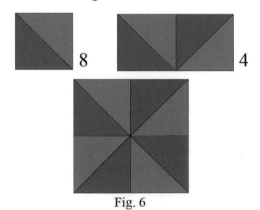

Fig. 6

9. **Block 4.** Sew a bright pink print 8⅝" HST to a 8⅝" wine print HST. Make 2 (Fig. 7).

Fig. 7

10. Arrange the 3 Block 3's and the 2 Block 4's as shown Fig. 10, B. Sew together.

11. Sew a 5⅞" green/beige print HST to a 5⅞" bright pink print HST. Make 7 (Fig. 8).

Fig. 8

12. Sew the 7 HST blocks together arranging blocks as shown in Fig. 9. Make 1 row.

Fig. 9

13. See the quilt layout in Fig. 10. Sew the green zebra print piece to the left edge of section A. Sew section B to the left edge. Sew a 38" green leopard skin print piece to the top and bottom edges. Sew the section C block strip to the bottom edge.

14. Sew a 53" red zebra print border piece to each side edge. Trim any excess border length allowing for a ¼" seam allowance.

15. Pin the 37" red zebra border pieces to the top and bottom edges and trim excess off allowing for a ¼" seam allowance. Sew a 2¾" wine print corner block to each end of the top and bottom border pieces, matching seams with the side borders. Sew borders.

16. Repeat to sew the dark pink small print borders pieces. Sew the 57" pieces to the side edges. Sew the 42" pieces to the top and bottom edges with the 3" green leopard skin corner blocks sewn to the top and bottom border pieces.

Fig. 10

Completing the quilt:

Follow the quilting instructions on page 62 to layer and quilt as desired. Our quilt was machine long arm quilted.

Follow the binding instructions on page 63 to attach the binding.

15

FINISHED QUILT SIZE - 50" X 60" (127 cm x 152 cm)

Fabric requirements:

The yardage requirement is based on 43" to 44" (109/112 cm) wide fabric.

- $^1/_2$ yd (46 cm) - bright green tonal fabric
- $^1/_2$ yd (46 cm) - light lavender print fabric
- $^3/_4$ yd (69 cm) - dark purple tonal fabric
- $^1/_2$ yard (46 cm) - blue tonal fabric
- $^1/_4$ yd (23 cm) - pale green/blue print fabric
- $1^1/_2$ yds (1.37 m) - purple large print fabric
- $^1/_2$ yd (46 cm) - green print fabric
- $^3/_8$ yd (34 cm) - white/purple large print fabric
- $^1/_4$ yd (23 cm) - purple small print fabric
- $^1/_2$ yd (46 cm) - fabric for binding
- $3^1/_2$ yds (3.20 m) - fabric for backing

You will also need:
58" x 68" (147 cm x 173 cm) piece of batting
Coordinating thread for quilting

Cutting the pieces:

Follow Rotary Cutting instructions on page 61 to cut the fabric. Cut pieces from selvage to selvage. The measurements include $^1/_4$" seam allowance. The borders and other long strip pieces are cut longer than necessary. Trim after sewing.

From the bight green tonal fabric:
Cut 2 side border pieces 2" x 52" (Cut and piece for 52").
Cut 2 top/bottom border pieces 2" x 46".

From the light lavender print fabric:
Cut 1 block $10^1/_4$" square. Cut diagonally twice for 4 quarter square triangles (QST's).

Cut 2 pieces $9^7/_8$" square. Cut diagonally for 4 half square triangles (HST's).
Cut 2 pieces $7^1/_4$" square. Cut diagonally twice for 8 QST's. (You will need to use 6 of the triangles.)
Cut 1 piece $4^1/_2$" x $6^1/_2$".
Cut 2 pieces $2^1/_4$" x $5^7/_8$".
Cut 2 pieces $2^1/_4$" x $4^1/_8$".

Cutting continued on page 18

16

Which Direction?

From the dark purple tonal fabric:
Cut 2 pieces $2\frac{1}{4}"$ x $7\frac{5}{8}"$
Cut 2 pieces $2\frac{1}{4}"$ x 4"
Cut 4 pieces $5\frac{7}{8}"$ square. Cut diagonally for 8 HST's.
Cut 4 pieces $5\frac{3}{8}"$ square. Cut diagonally for 8 HST's.
Cut 4 pieces $4\frac{7}{8}"$ square. Cut diagonally for 8 HST's.
Cut 18 pieces $3\frac{7}{8}"$ square. Cut diagonally for 36 HST's.

From the blue tonal fabric:
Cut 2 pieces $2\frac{1}{2}"$ x 42".
Cut 1 piece $2\frac{1}{2}"$ x $12\frac{1}{2}"$.

From the pale green/blue print fabric:
Cut 2 pieces $5\frac{7}{8}"$ square. Cut diagonally for 4 HST's.
Cut 1 piece $1\frac{1}{2}"$ x $18\frac{1}{2}"$.

From the purple large print fabric:
Cut 2 side border pieces 4" x 56" (Cut and piece for 56").
Cut 2 top/bottom border pieces 4" x 53" (Cut and piece for 53").
Cut 2 pieces $7\frac{5}{8}"$ square.
Cut 3 pieces $7\frac{1}{4}"$ square. Cut diagonally twice for 12 QST's.
Cut 2 pieces $5\frac{7}{8}"$ square. Cut diagonally for 4 HST's.
Cut 1 piece $5\frac{3}{4}"$ square. Cut diagonally twice for 4 QST's.
Cut 1 piece 5" square.
Cut 4 pieces $4\frac{7}{8}"$ square. Cut diagonally for 8 HST's.
Cut 1 piece 4" square.

From the green print fabric:
Cut 1 block $10\frac{1}{4}"$ square. Cut diagonally twice for 4 QST's.
Cut 2 pieces $9\frac{7}{8}"$ square. Cut diagonally for 4 HST's.
Cut 4 pieces $4\frac{7}{8}"$ square. Cut diagonally for 8 HST's (You will need only 7 HST's).
Cut 2 pieces $2\frac{1}{4}"$ x $7\frac{3}{4}"$.
Cut 2 pieces $2\frac{1}{4}"$ x $5\frac{7}{8}"$.

From the white/purple large print fabric:
Cut 1 piece $5\frac{3}{4}"$ square. Cut diagonally twice for 4 QST's.
Cut 1 piece 5" square.
Cut 4 pieces $4\frac{7}{8}"$ square. Cut diagonally for 8 HST's (you will need only 7 HST's).
Cut 2 pieces $2\frac{1}{4}"$ x $9\frac{1}{2}"$.
Cut 2 pieces $2\frac{1}{4}"$ x $7\frac{3}{4}"$.

From the purple small print fabric:
Cut 2 pieces $5\frac{7}{8}"$ square. Cut diagonally for 4 HST's.
Cut 2 pieces $4\frac{1}{8}"$ square.

For the binding:
Cut 6 strips $2\frac{1}{2}"$ x width of fabric.

Assembling the quilt top:

Sew all pieces right sides together and sew with a $\frac{1}{4}"$ seam allowance. Press all seams as you sew, pressing the seams toward the darker fabric.

1. **Block 1.** Make 2 blocks with alternating fabrics. See Fig. 1 for sewing the block, starting with the center block and adding HST's/QST's working outward. Sew triangles to 2 opposite edges first, then to the remaining 2 edges.

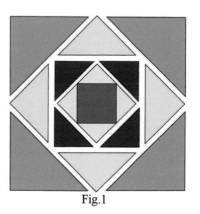

Fig.1

2. **Block 1A.** Sew a $5\frac{3}{4}"$ white/purple QST to 2 opposite edges of a 5" purple large print square piece then to the other 2 edges of the block. Sew the following triangle pieces in this order - $5\frac{3}{8}"$ purple tonal HST's, $10\frac{1}{4}"$ green print QST's and $9\frac{7}{8}"$ light lavender print HST's. Make 1 block.

3. **Block 1B.** Sew a $5\frac{3}{4}"$ purple large print QST to 2 opposite edges of a 5" white/purple square block then to the other 2 edges of the block. Sew the following triangle pieces in this order - $5\frac{3}{8}"$ purple tonal HST's, $10\frac{1}{4}"$ light lavender print QST's and $9\frac{7}{8}"$ green print HST's. Make 1 block.

4. **Block 2.** Sew a $4\frac{7}{8}"$ green print HST to a $4\frac{7}{8}"$ white/purple HST. Make 7. Sew 2 blocks together arranging the blocks as shown in Fig. 2 below. Make 3. 1 block will remain single.

19

5. Sew a 4⅞" purple tonal HST to a 4⅞" purple large print HST. Make 8. Sew 2 HST blocks together. Make 2 two-block units in each arrangement in Fig. 2.

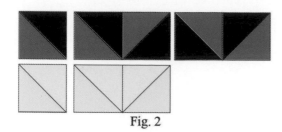

Fig. 2

6. Sew 2 two-HST purple block units together. Make 2 blocks, 1 block in each direction as shown in Fig. 3 below.

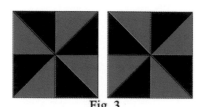

Fig. 3

7. Sew a green/white HST two-block unit to the bottom edge of 1 purple block and another unit to the top edge of the other purple block. Sew the single green/white HST block to the end of the remaining two-block unit. See the Fig. 4 for block arrangement. Sew the blocks units together. Sew the 2½" x 12½" blue tonal piece to the left edge.

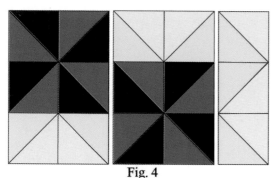

Fig. 4

8. **Block 3**. Sew a 3⅞" purple tonal HST to each diagonal edge of a 7¼" purple large print QST. Make 12 (Fig 5). Sew 6 blocks together. Make 2 rows.

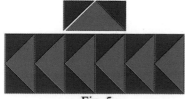

Fig. 5

9. Sew a 3⅞" purple tonal HST to each diagonal edge of a 7¼" light lavender print QST. Make 6. Sew 3 blocks together. Make 2 rows. Turning the 2 rows pointed in opposite directions, sew 1 row to each side of the 4½" x 6½" light lavender piece (Fig 6).

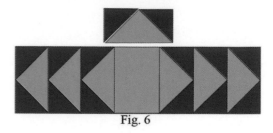

Fig. 6

10. **Block 4**. See Fig. 7 for the sewing arrangement. Make 2 blocks. Sew pieces, adding to the 4⅛" block in the following order:
- Sew a 2½" x 4⅛" light lavender piece the bottom edge of a 4⅛" square purple small print piece.
- Sew a 5⅞" light lavender piece to the left edge.
- Sew a 5⅞" green print piece to the bottom edge.
- Sew a 7¾" green piece to the left edge.
- Sew a 7¾" white/purple print to the bottom edge.
- Sew a 9½" white purple print to the left edge.

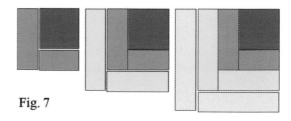

Fig. 7

11. Sew the 2 blocks together, sewing the edges with the purple small print blocks. See the quilt layout Fig. 11, Section E. Sew the 1½" x 18½" pale green/blue print piece to a side edge.

12. **Block 5.** Sew a 5⅞" purple tonal HST to 2 opposite edges of a 7⅞" purple large print square piece. Sew a purple tonal HST to the remaining 2 edges (Fig. 8). Make 2.

Fig. 8

13. **Block 6.** Sew a 2¼" x 4" purple tonal piece to 2 opposite edges of a 4" purple large print square piece. Sew a 2¼" x 7⅝" purple tonal piece to each side edge. Make 1. Sew a 5⅞"

purple large print HST to 2 opposite edges. Sew the 2 remaining HST's to the other 2 edges.

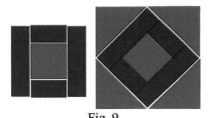

Fig. 9

14. **Block 7.** Sew a $5\frac{7}{8}$" purple small print HST to a $5\frac{7}{8}$" pale green/blue print HST. Make 4. Sew 2 HST blocks together as shown in Fig. 10. Make 2. Sew the 2 two-block units together. Make 1 block.

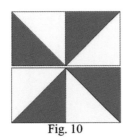

Fig. 10

15. Sew blocks 5, 6 and 7 together to form a row. See the arrangement for the blocks in the quilt layout Fig. 11, section D below.

16. See Fig. 11 for sewing all the units together in the following order:
- Sew section C to the bottom of section B.
- Sew block A to the left edge of the B/C section.
- Sew a 42" blue tonal piece to the bottom edge of the A/B/C section.
- Sew section D to the bottom edge.
- Sew a 42" blue tonal piece to the bottom edge of section D.
- Sew a section F to the left edge of block G. Arrange with the points turned down.
- Sew a section F to the right edge of block G. Arrange with the points turned up.
- Sew section E to the left edge of the F/G section.
- Sew the E, F, G section to the bottom edge of the blue tonal piece.

17. Sew a 52" bright green tonal border piece to each side edge. Sew a 46" bright green tonal border piece to the top and bottom edges.

18. Sew a 56" purple border piece to each side edge. Sew a 53" purple border piece to the top and bottom edges.

Fig. 11

Completing the quilt:

Follow the quilting instructions on page 62 to layer and quilt as desired. Our quilt was machine long arm quilted.

Follow the binding instructions on page 63 to attach the binding.

21

FINISHED QUILT SIZE - 52¹/₄" x 68¹/₂" (133 cm x 174 cm)
FINISHED BLOCK SIZE - 10¹/₄" x 10¹/₄" (26 cm x 26 cm)

Fabric requirements:

The yardage requirement is based on 43" to 44" (109/112 cm) wide fabric.

- ¹/₂ yd (46 cm) - bright pink tonal fabric
- ¹/₂ yd (46 cm) - yellow print fabric
- ³/₄ yd (69 cm) - green plaid fabric
- ³/₄ yd (69 cm) - blue print fabric
- ³/₄ yd (69 cm) - pink stripe fabric
- ³/₄ yd (69 cm) - bright green print fabric
- 1³/₄ yd (1.60 m) - green multicolor border fabric
- ¹/₂ yd (46 cm) - fabric for binding
- 3¹/₂ yds (3.20 m) - fabric for backing

You will also need:
60" x 76" (152 cm x 193 cm) piece of backing
Coordinating thread for quilting

Illusions

Cutting the pieces:

Follow Rotary Cutting instructions on page 61 to cut the fabric. Cut pieces from selvage to selvage. The measurements include ¼" seam allowance. The borders are cut longer than necessary. Trim after sewing.

From the bright pink tonal fabric:
Cut 2 blocks 9⅛" square. Cut blocks diagonally for 4 half square triangles (HST's).
Cut 4 blocks 6" square. Cut blocks diagonally for 8 HST's.
Cut 2 pieces 2⅜" x 8⅞".
Cut 2 pieces 2⅜" x 7".

From the yellow print fabric:
Cut 2 blocks 11½" square. Cut diagonally twice for 8 quarter square triangles (QST's).

Cut 4 blocks 4⅛" square. Cut diagonally for 8 HST's.

From the green plaid fabric:
Cut 2 blocks 11½" square. Cut diagonally twice for 8 QST's.
Cut 2 blocks 9⅛" square. Cut blocks diagonally for 4 HST's.
Cut 2 pieces 2⅜" x 10¾". Fussy cut if using plaid fabric to align plaid with pieces below.
Cut 2 pieces 2⅜" x 8⅞".

From the blue print fabric:
Cut 2 top/bottom border pieces 3½" x 38".
Cut 1 block 7⅜" square. Cut diagonally for 2 HST's.
Cut 8 pieces 2⅜" x 6".

From the pink stripe fabric:
Cut 4 blocks 11½" square. Cut diagonally twice for 16 QST's.

From the bright green print fabric:
Cut 2 side border pieces 3" x 43"
Cut 2 top/bottom border pieces 3" x 38".
Cut 1 block 7⅜" square. Cut diagonally for 2 HST's.

From the green multicolor border fabric:
Cut 2 side border pieces 8¾" x 54". Fussy cut if using border fabric. (Cut and piece to get 54".)
Cut 2 top/bottom border pieces 8¾" x 38". Fussy cut if using border fabric.

For the binding:
Cut 6 strips 2½" x width of fabric.

Assembling the quilt top:

Sew all pieces right sides together and sew with a ¼" seam allowance. Press all seams as you sew, pressing the seams toward the darker fabric.

1. **Block 1**. Sew a 7⅜" bright green print HST to a 7⅜" blue print HST (Fig. 1, A). Make 2. Sew a 7" bright pink piece to the green edge (Fig. 1, B). Sew a 8⅞" bright pink piece to an adjacent side edge. Make 2. Sew an 8⅞" green plaid piece to the top edge and a 10¾" green plaid piece to the side edge (Fig. 1, C). Make 2 blocks.

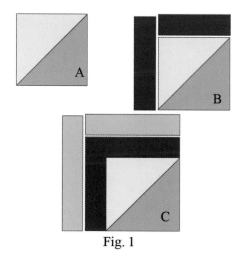

Fig. 1

2. **Block 2**. Sew a 2⅜" x 6" blue print piece to a 4⅛" yellow print HST. Trim the end of the blue piece as shown in Fig. 2. Sew to a 6" bright pink HST (Fig. 2). Make 8 blocks.

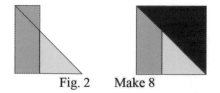

Fig. 2   Make 8

3. Sew 2 HST blocks together arranged as shown Fig. 3. Make 4. Sew 2 of the two-block units together. Make 2 blocks.

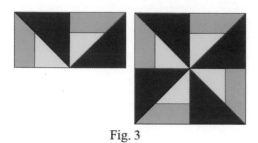

Fig. 3

4. **Block 3 corner block**. Sew a $9\frac{1}{8}$" bright pink HST to a $9\frac{1}{8}$" green plaid HST (Fig. 4). Make 4.

Fig. 4

5. **Block 4**. Sew a $11\frac{1}{2}$" yellow print QST to a $11\frac{1}{2}$" green plaid QST. Make 8. Sew 2 QST blocks together arranged as shown in Fig. 5. Make 4.

 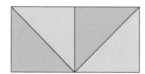

Fig. 5

6. Sew 2 two-block units together (Fig. 6). Make 2 blocks.

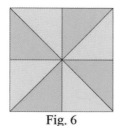

Fig. 6

7. Sew two $11\frac{1}{2}$" stripe QST pieces together. Make 8 in 2 arrangements. Sew 4 arranged with the stripes in one direction and sew 4 with the stripes arranged in the opposite direction as shown in Fig. 7. Match stripes.

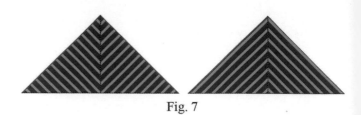

Fig. 7

8. Sew 2 matching QST units to 2 opposite edges of a green/yellow QST block unit. Sew the remaining 2 matching QST units to the other 2 edges. Make a second block using the remaining 4 stripe QST units and the second green/yellow QST block. See Fig. 8 for the positioning of the stripes and arrangement for each block.

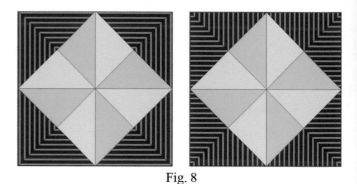

Fig. 8

9. See Fig. 9 for the quilt layout below for arranging blocks.
- Sew Block 1 to Block 2. Make 2.
- Sew a Block 1/Block 2 unit to a side edge of Block 4. Make 2. Sew the 2 units together.

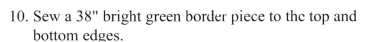

Fig. 9

Fig. 10

10. Sew a 38" bright green border piece to the top and bottom edges.

11. Sew a 43" bright green border piece to each side edge. Trim ends.

12. Sew a 38" blue print border piece to the top and bottom edges.

13. Sew a 54" green multicolor border piece to the side edges.

14. Pin a 38" green multicolor border piece to the top and bottom edges and trim excess off allowing for a $1/4$" seam allowance. Sew a bright pink/green plaid HST corner blocks to each end of the top and bottom border strips, matching seams with the side borders. Arrange corner blocks with the green plaid edges sewn to the border pieces (see Fig. 10). Sew borders.

Completing the quilt:

Follow the quilting instructions on page 62 to layer and quilt as desired. Our quilt was machine long arm quilted.

Follow the binding instructions on page 63 to attach the binding.

FINISHED QUILT SIZE - 46" x 63" (117 cm x 160 cm)
FINISHED BLOCK SIZE - 10" x 10" (25 cm x 25 cm)

Fabric requirements:

The yardage requirement is based on 43" to 44" (109/112 cm) wide fabric.

- $^1/_4$ yd (23 cm) - purple floral print fabric
- $^5/_8$ yd (57 cm) - dark green print fabric
- $^3/_8$ yd (34 cm) - pale green geometric print fabric
- $^1/_4$ yd (23 cm) - beige with green print fabric
- $^3/_8$ yd (34 cm) - beige with purple print fabric
- $^3/_8$ yd (34 cm) - stripe fabric
- $^3/_4$ yd (69 cm) - dark green tonal fabric
- $^1/_4$ yd (23 cm) - pale lavender geometric print fabric
- $^1/_2$ yd (46 cm) - purple small floral print fabric
- 1 yd (91 cm) - green floral print fabric
- $^3/_4$ yd (69 cm) - dark purple print fabric
- $^1/_2$ yd (46 cm) - fabric for binding
- 3 yds (2.75 m) - fabric for backing

You will also need:
54" x 71" (137 cm x 180 cm) piece of batting
Fusible web with paper backing
Coordinating thread for quilting

Cutting the pieces:

Follow Rotary Cutting instructions on page 61 to cut the fabric. Cut pieces from selvage to selvage. The measurements include ¼" seam allowance. The borders and long strip pieces are cut longer than necessary. Trim after sewing.

See page 62 for instructions on cutting the fusible web appliqué pieces.

From the purple floral print fabric:

Cut 2 pieces 7⅝" square.
Cut 2 pieces 5⅞" square. Cut diagonally for 4 half square triangles (HST's).
Cut 4 pieces 3½" square for border corner blocks.

Cutting continued on page 30

Floral Majesty

From the dark green print fabric:
Cut 8 pieces 5⁷⁄₈" square. Cut diagonally for 16 HST's.
Cut 2 pieces 2⁵⁄₈" x 7⁵⁄₈".
Cut 2 pieces 2⁵⁄₈" x 3³⁄₈".
Cut 1 leaf (reverse the leaf pattern) and 1 stem for appliqué using the patterns on page 35. (See page 62 for directions on cutting fusible web appliqué.)

Cut from pale green geometric print fabric:
(If the fabric has a direction, cut half the HST's one direction and the other half the opposite direction. Turn the square piece diagonal.)
Cut 2 pieces 10⁷⁄₈" square. Cut diagonally for 4 HST's.
Cut 2 pieces 7⁷⁄₈" square. Cut diagonally for 4 HST's.
Cut 1 piece 3³⁄₈" square.

From beige/green print fabric:
Cut 2 pieces 5⁷⁄₈" square. Cut diagonally for 4 HST's.

From beige/purple print fabric:
Cut 4 pieces 5⁷⁄₈" square. Cut diagonally for 8 HST's.
Cut flower centers for appliqué using the pattern on page 34. Enlarge the pieces based on the percentages given for each flower.

From stripe fabric:
Cut 1 piece 3¹⁄₂" x 43".
Cut 2 pieces 2¹⁄₂" x 43".

From dark green tonal fabric:
Cut 2 side border pieces 3¹⁄₂" x 60" (Cut and piece for 60").
Cut 2 top/bottom border pieces 3¹⁄₂" x 43".
Cut 2 pieces 2⁵⁄₈" x 7⁵⁄₈".
Cut 2 pieces 2⁵⁄₈" x 3³⁄₈".
Cut 1 piece 3³⁄₈" square.
Cut 1 leaf for appliqué using the patterns on pages 35.

From pale lavender geometric print fabric:
(If the fabric has a direction, cut half the HST's one direction and the other half the opposite direction. Turn the square piece and cut diagonal.)
Cut 1 piece 7⁵⁄₈" square.
Cut 4 pieces 5⁷⁄₈" square. Cut diagonally for 8 HST's.

From purple small floral print fabric:
Cut 3 pieces 7⁵⁄₈" square.
Cut 2 pieces 5⁷⁄₈" square. Cut diagonally for 4 HST's.
Cut 1 piece 3³⁄₈" square.
Cut 4 pieces 2⁵⁄₈" x 15³⁄₈". Cut ends diagonally at a 45° angle.

From green floral print fabric:
Cut 4 pieces 10⁷⁄₈" square. Cut diagonally for 8 HST's.
Cut 2 pieces 5⁷⁄₈" square. Cut diagonally for 4 HST's.
Cut 2 pieces 2⁵⁄₈" x 7⁵⁄₈".
Cut 2 pieces 2⁵⁄₈" x 3³⁄₈".

From dark purple print fabric:
Cut 2 pieces 7⁵⁄₈" square.
Cut 2 pieces 2⁵⁄₈" x 7⁵⁄₈".
Cut 2 pieces 2⁵⁄₈" x 3³⁄₈".
Cut 1 piece 3³⁄₈" square.
Cut 1 flower each size for appliqué 14", 12" and 8".
See pattern on page 34. Enlarge the pieces based on the percentages given for each flower.

For the Binding:
Cut 6 strips 2¹⁄₂" x width of fabric.

Assembling the quilt top:

Sew all pieces right sides together and sew with a ¹⁄₄" seam allowance. Press all seams as you sew, pressing the seams toward the darker fabric.

1. **Block 1.** 8 blocks are made with different fabric combinations as listed below. For each block, sew a 5⁷⁄₈" HST to 2 opposite edges of a 7⁵⁄₈" square piece. Sew a HST to the remaining 2 edges. (Fig. 1)

31

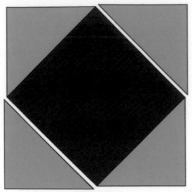

Fig. 1

2. Make 8 blocks in the following combinations with $7^5/_8$" square blocks and $5^7/_8$" HST's:

- 3 blocks - block from purple small floral print and HST's from dark green print.
- 1 block - block from pale lavender geometric fabric and HST's from purple floral print.
- 1 block - block from dark purple print and HST's from beige with green print.
- 1 block - block from dark purple print and HST's from beige with purple print.
- 1 block - block from purple floral print with HST's from green floral print.
- 1 block - block from purple floral print with HST's from pale lavender geometric print.

3. **Block 2**. Sew a $10^7/_8$" green floral print HST to a $10^7/_8$" pale green geometric print HST. Make 4 blocks (Fig. 2).

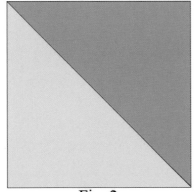

Fig. 2

4. **Block 3**. Sew a $15^3/_8$" purple small floral print piece to the a $7^7/_8$" pale green geometric print HST. Make 4. Sew a $10^7/_8$" green floral print HST to the triangle unit. Make 4 blocks (Fig. 3).

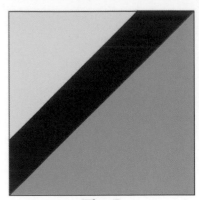

Fig. 3

5. **Block 4**. Make 4 blocks with the different fabric combinations listed below. Sew a $2^5/_8$" x $3^3/_8$" piece to 2 opposite edges of a $3^3/_8$" square block. Sew a $2^5/_8$" x $7^5/_8$" piece to the remaining 2 edges. Sew a $5^7/_8$" HST to 2 opposite sides. Sew a $5^7/_8$" HST to the remaining 2 sides (Fig. 4).

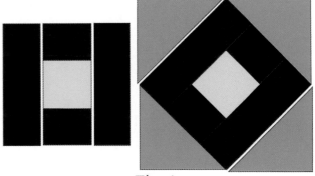

Fig. 4

6. Make 4 blocks in the following combinations:

- 1 block - dark green tonal block center, green floral print side pieces and purple small floral print HST's.
- 1 block - pale green geometric block center, dark purple print side pieces and dark green print HST's.
- 1 block - purple small floral block center, dark green print side pieces and pale lavender geometric HST's.
- 1 block - dark purple print block center, dark green tonal side pieces and beige with purple HST's.

7. See Fig. 5 for the quilt block arrangement. Sew 4 blocks in rows as shown. Sew the top 3 rows and sew the $3^1/_2$" wide stripe piece to the bottom edge. Sew the remaining 2 rows of blocks and sew to the bottom edge of the stripe piece. Sew a $2^1/_2$" wide stripe piece to the top and bottom edges.

Fig. 5

8. See the appliqué instructions on page 62. Fuse and appliqué the flower centers on the flowers. Arrange the appliqué pieces on the quilt top. Place the top end of the stem under the flower and the end of the leaf stems under the flower and stem. Fuse and appliqué the stem, leaves and flowers.

9. Sew a 60" dark green tonal border piece to each side edge. Trim any excess border length allowing for a $^1/_4$" seam allowance.

10. Pin the 43" stripe border strips to the top and bottom edges. Trim excess off allowing for a $^1/_4$" seam allowance. Sew a $3^1/_2$" square corner block to each end of the top and bottom border strips, matching seams with the side borders. Sew borders.

Completing the quilt:

Follow the quilting instructions on page 62 to layer and quilt as desired. Our quilt was machine long arm quilted.

Follow the binding instructions on page 63 to attach the binding.

FLORAL MAJESTY QUILT PATTERN
Small flower pattern
For medium size flower pattern - enlarge 150%
For large size flower pattern - enlarge 175%

Permission granted to
photocopy for purposes
of enlargement and use
in making this quilt.

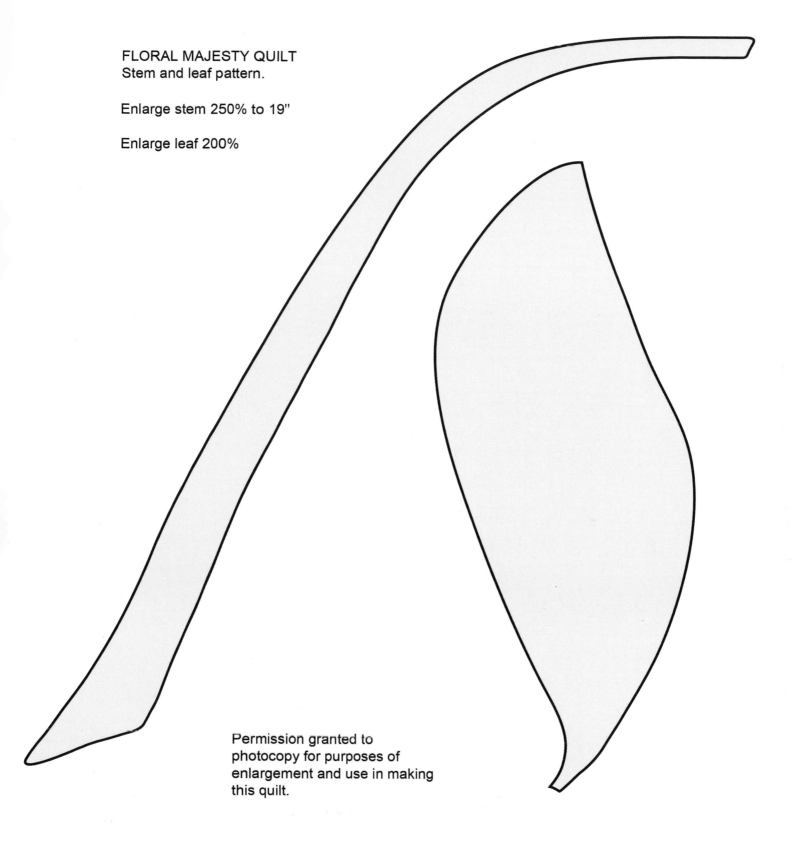

FLORAL MAJESTY QUILT
Stem and leaf pattern.

Enlarge stem 250% to 19"

Enlarge leaf 200%

Permission granted to
photocopy for purposes of
enlargement and use in making
this quilt.

Finished Quilt Size - 46¹/₂" x 63¹/₂" (118 cm x 161 cm)
Finished Block Size - 14¹/₂" x 14¹/₂" (37 cm x 37 cm)

Fabric requirements:

The yardage requirement is based on 43" to 44" (109/112 cm) wide fabric.

- 1¹/₄ yds (1.14 m) - yellow tonal fabric
- ¹/₂ yd (46 cm) - turquoise tonal fabric
- 1 yd (91 cm) - green print fabric
- ¹/₂ yd (46 cm) - pink multicolor large print fabric
- ¹/₄ yd (23 cm) - black multicolor small print fabric
- ¹/₈ yd (12 cm) - white paisley print fabric
- ¹/₄ yd (23 cm) - white/pink multicolor small print fabric
- ¹/₄ yd (23 cm) - purple print fabric
- ¹/₂ yd (46 cm) - stripe fabric
- ¹/₂ yd (46 cm) - fabric for binding
- 3¹/₄ yds (2.97 m) - fabric for backing

You will also need:
56" x 75" (142 cm x 191 cm) piece of batting
Coordinating thread for quilting

Cutting the pieces:

Follow Rotary Cutting instructions on page 61 to cut the fabric. Cut pieces from selvage to selvage. The measurements include ¹/₄" seam allowance. The borders are cut longer than necessary. Trim after sewing.

From the yellow tonal fabric:
Cut 2 side border pieces 3" x 56".
Cut 3 top/bottom border and sashing pieces 3" x 34".
Cut 1 sashing piece 3" x 19".
Cut 3 sashing pieces 3" x 15".
Cut 6 pieces using the pattern on page 60.
Cut 6 blocks 8¹/₂" x 4⁵/₈". Cut 3 blocks diagonally one direction and 3 blocks diagonally the opposite direction. See Fig. 1 and Fig. 2.

Fig. 1

Fig. 2

Cutting continued on page 38

Tilt A Whirl

From the turquoise tonal fabric:
Cut 2 blocks $8\frac{1}{2}$" x $4\frac{5}{8}$". Cut diagonally in the direction shown in Fig. 2 for 4 pieces (You will need to use only 3 pieces).

Fig. 2

Cut 1 piece $5\frac{7}{8}$" x $4\frac{1}{8}$".
Cut 8 blocks $4\frac{1}{2}$" square. Cut in half diagonally for 16 half square triangles (HST's).
Cut 1 piece $1\frac{3}{4}$" x 15".
Cut 4 border corner blocks $3\frac{1}{2}$" square.

From the green print fabric:
Cut 2 side border pieces $2\frac{1}{2}$" x 60".
Cut 2 top and bottom border pieces $2\frac{1}{2}$" x 49".
Cut 1 sashing piece 3" x 15".
Cut 3 pieces using the pattern on page 60.
Cut 2 pieces $5\frac{7}{8}$" x $4\frac{1}{8}$".
Cut 4 blocks $4\frac{1}{2}$" square. Cut in half diagonally for 8 HST's.

From the pink multicolor large print fabric:
Cut 1 piece 15" x $7\frac{3}{4}$".
Cut 8 blocks $4\frac{1}{2}$" square. Cut in half diagonally for 16 HST's.
Cut 3 pieces using the pattern on page 60.

From the black multicolor small print fabric:
Cut 2 pieces $1\frac{1}{8}$" x 15"
Cut 1 piece $1\frac{3}{4}$" x 15"
Cut 1 piece $5\frac{7}{8}$" x $4\frac{1}{8}$"
Cut 2 blocks $8\frac{1}{2}$" x $4\frac{5}{8}$". Cut diagonally the direction shown in Fig. 1 for 4 pieces (You will need to use only 3 pieces).

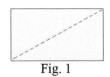

Fig. 1

From the white paisley print fabric:
Cut 4 blocks $4\frac{1}{2}$" square. Cut in half diagonally for 8 HST's.
Cut 2 pieces $5\frac{7}{8}$" x $4\frac{1}{8}$".

From the white/pink multicolor small print fabric:
Cut 2 blocks $8\frac{1}{2}$" x $4\frac{5}{8}$". Cut diagonally the direction shown in Fig. 2 for 4 pieces (You will need to use only 3 pieces).

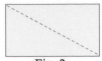

Fig. 2

From the purple print fabric:
Cut 2 pieces $5\frac{7}{8}$" x $4\frac{1}{8}$"
Cut 2 blocks $8\frac{1}{2}$" x $4\frac{5}{8}$". Cut diagonally the direction shown in Fig. 1 for 4 pieces (You will need to use only 3 pieces).

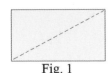

Fig. 1

From the stripe fabric:
Cut 2 side border pieces $3\frac{1}{2}$" x 57" (Cut and piece for 57")
Cut 2 top and bottom border pieces $3\frac{1}{2}$" x 39"

For the binding:
Cut 6 strips $2\frac{1}{2}$" x width of fabric.

Assembling the quilt top:

Sew all pieces right sides together and sew with a $\frac{1}{4}$" seam allowance. Press all seams as you sew, pressing the seams toward the darker fabric.

1. **Block 1.** Using the pieces cut with the pattern, sew a $8\frac{1}{2}$" triangular piece to each long side edge of the piece cut with the pattern following the directions below for arrangement (Fig. 3).

Fig. 3

Sew 3 units of each of the following combination:

- Sew a multicolor black print piece and a turquoise print piece to the side edges of a yellow pattern piece.
- Sew a yellow piece to each side edge of a pink multicolor print pattern piece.
- Sew a yellow piece to each side edge of a green print pattern piece.
- Sew a white/pink multicolor piece and a purple piece to the side edges of a yellow pattern piece.

2. Sew the block with the yellow, aqua and black fabrics to the block with the yellow and pink multicolor fabrics. Make 3. Sew the block with the yellow and green fabrics to the block with the yellow, purple and white/pink multicolor fabrics. Make 3. See diagram in Fig. 4 for block arrangements for sewing. Sew the 2 block units together. (Fig. 4) Make 3 blocks.

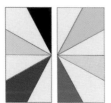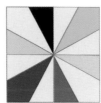

Fig. 4

3. **Block 2.** Sew 2 blocks in 2 different color combinations, 1 in each combination. Sew a $4^{1}/_{2}$" turquoise HST to a $4^{1}/_{2}$" pink multicolor HST. Sew a $4^{1}/_{2}$" green print HST to a $4^{1}/_{2}$" pink multicolor HST (Fig. 5). Make 8 of each.

Fig. 5   Make 8 of Each

4. Sew 4 blocks of each combination together (Fig. 6). Make 2 rows with each block combination.

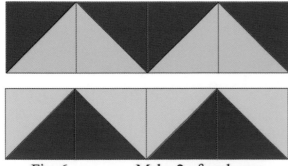

Fig. 6   Make 2 of each row

5. Sew 4 of the $5^{7}/_{8}$" x $4^{1}/_{8}$" pieces together on the $5^{7}/_{8}$" edge (Fig. 7). Sew the green, black multicolor, purple and white/pink multicolor pieces together. Sew a second unit, sewing the purple, white paisley, turquoise and green pieces together.

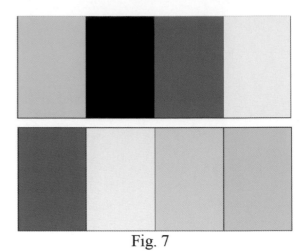

Fig. 7

6. Sew the HST block rows from number 4 together, turning the rows in opposite directions and joining with a black multicolor $1^{1}/_{8}$" x 15" piece. (Fig. 8.) Sew the block rows created in number 5 together, joining with the $1^{3}/_{4}$" x 15" turquoise and black multicolor pieces. Arrange blocks as shown in Fig. 8.

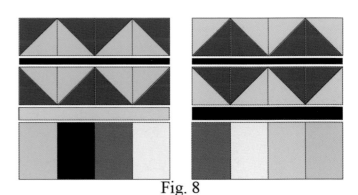

Fig. 8

7. **Block 3**. Sew a turquoise HST to a white paisley HST. Make 8. Sew 4 blocks together as shown in Fig. 9. Make 2 rows.

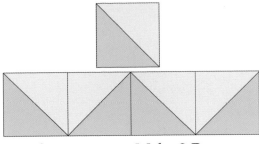

Fig. 9   Make 2 Rows

8. Sew a HST row to each long side edge of the 15" x 7³/₄" pink multicolor piece. See Fig. 10 for directional arrangement of the HST block rows.

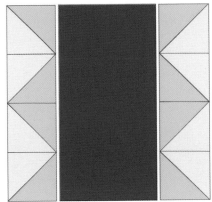

Fig. 10

9. Sew the 15" green sashing piece to the end of the 19" yellow sashing piece (Fig. 11).

Fig. 11

10. See Fig. 12 for block arrangement for sewing. Sew 2 blocks together joining with the 3" x 15" yellow sashing pieces. Make 3 rows. Sew the top 2 rows together with the 34" yellow and green sashing piece and join the bottom row with a 34" yellow sashing piece. Sew a 34" yellow piece to the top and bottom edges.

11. Sew a 56" yellow piece to each side edge.

12. Sew a 57" stripe border piece to each side edge. Trim off excess allowing for a ¹/₄" seam allowance.

13. Pin the 39" stripe border strips to the top and bottom edges and trim excess off allowing for a ¹/₄" seam allowance. Sew a 3¹/₂" turquoise corner block to each end of the top and bottom border pieces, matching seams with the side borders. Sew borders.

14. Sew a 60" green print border pieces to each side edge. Sew the 47" green print border pieces to the top and bottom edges.

Fig. 12

Completing the quilt:

Follow the quilting instructions on page 62 to layer and quilt as desired. Our quilt was machine long arm quilted.
Follow the binding instructions on page 63 to attach the binding.

41

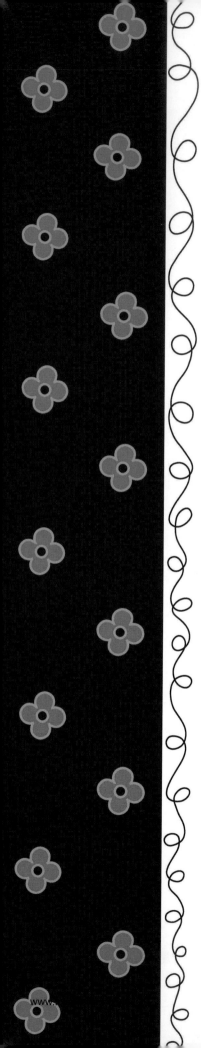

Finished Quilt Size - 57" x 66¹/₂" (145 cm x 169 cm)
Finished Block size - 9" x 9" (23 cm x 23 cm)

Fabric requirements:

The yardage requirement is based on 43" to 44" (109/112 cm) wide fabric.

- 1¹/₂ yds (1.37 m) - yellow print fabric
- ⁷/₈ yd (80 cm) - green print fabric
- ¹/₄ yd (23 cm) - stripe fabric
- ³/₈ yd (34 cm) - blue tonal fabric
- 1¹/₄ yd (1.14 m) - small red print fabric
- 1/4 yd (23 cm) - small blue print fabric
- 1 yd (91 cm) - light red tonal fabric
- 1/2 yd (46 cm) - fabric for binding
- 3³/₄ yds (3.43 m) - fabric for backing

You will also need:
65" x 75" (165 cm x 191 cm) piece of batting
Coordinating thread for quilting

Cutting the pieces:

Follow Rotary Cutting instructions on page 61 to cut the fabric. Cut pieces from selvage to selvage. The measurements include ¹/₄" seam allowance. The borders are cut longer than necessary. Trim after sewing.

Due to the large number of pieces for this quilt with many blocks and triangles being very similar in size, it is suggested that you label each set of pieces as you cut them. This will make it easier when sewing and prevent possible errors in piecing.

From the yellow print fabric:
Cut 29 blocks 5³/₈" square. Cut diagonally for 58 half square triangles (HST's).
Cut 8 blocks 5³/₄" square. Cut diagonally twice for 32 quarter square triangles (QST's).

Cut 12 blocks 4¹/₄" square. Cut diagonally twice for 48 QST's.
Cut 16 blocks 3¹/₈" square. Cut diagonally for 32 HST's.
Cut 8 blocks 2³/₈" square. Cut diagonally for 16 HST's.
Cut 32 blocks 2¹/₈" square.

Cutting continued on page 44

Swirling Stars

From the green print fabric:
Cut 2 side border pieces 2" x 61" (Cut and piece for 61").
Cut 2 top/bottom border pieces 2" x 55" (Cut and piece for 55").
Cut 4 pieces $2^5/_8$" x width of fabric. Cut into 64 blocks $2^5/_8$" square.

From the stripe fabric:
Cut 2 pieces $2^3/_4$" x 38".

From the blue tonal fabric:
Cut 2 pieces $2^1/_2$" x 62" (Cut and piece for 62").

From the small red print fabric:
Cut 2 side border pieces 3" x 64" (Cut and piece for 64").
Cut 2 top/bottom border pieces 3" x 60" (Cut and piece for 60").
Cut 4 blocks $10^1/_4$" square. Cut diagonally twice for 16 QST's (You will need to use only 13 of the triangles).
Cut 4 blocks $4^1/_4$" square. Cut diagonally twice for 16 QST's.
Cut 8 blocks $2^5/_8$" square.
Cut 8 blocks $2^3/_8$" square. Cut diagonally for 16 HST's.

From the small blue print fabric:
Cut 32 blocks $2^5/_8$" square.

From the light red tonal fabric:
Cut 16 blocks $5^3/_8$" square. Cut diagonally for 32 HST's.
Cut 8 blocks $5^3/_4$" square. Cut diagonally twice for 32 QST's.
Cut 16 blocks $3^1/_8$" square. Cut diagonally for 32 HST's.
Cut 32 blocks $2^1/_8$" square.

For the binding:
Cut $6^1/_2$ strips $2^1/_2$" x width of fabric.

Assembling the quilt top:

Sew all pieces right sides together and sew with a $^1/_4$" seam allowance. Press all seams as you sew, pressing the seams toward the darker fabric.

1. **Block 1** - Sewing the stars. Sew using 32 pieces each for the following pieces:
- $5^3/_8$" HST's from the light red and yellow fabrics
- $3^1/_8$" HST's from the light red and yellow fabrics
- $5^3/_4$" QST's from the light red and yellow fabrics
- $2^1/_8$" squares from the light red and yellow fabrics

2. Sew a $2^1/_8$" light red square to a $2^1/_8$" yellow square. Make 16. Sew 2 two-block units together. Make 8 blocks (Fig. 1)

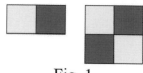

Fig. 1

3. See Fig. 2 below for the color arrangement for sewing the pieces. Sew 2 light red $3^1/_8$" HST's to opposite sides of the block. Sew 2 yellow $3^1/_8$" HST's to the remaining 2 sides.

4. Sew 2 light red $5^3/_4$" QST's to 2 opposite sides of the block. Sew 2 yellow $5^3/_4$" QST's to the remaining 2 sides.

5. Sew 2 light red $5^3/_8$" HST's to 2 opposite sides of the block. Sew 2 yellow $5^3/_8$" HST's to the remaining 2 sides.

Fig. 2

6. Sew 4 blocks together, arranging the blocks for each row as shown in Fig. 3. Sew 4 rows then sew rows together.

Fig. 3

Fig. 5

7. **Block 2.** Sew using the following pieces:
- 26 yellow $5^3/8$" HST's
- 13 red print $10^1/4$" QST's.

8. Sew a yellow HST to each diagonal edge of the red triangle. Make 13.

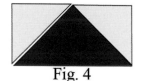

Fig. 4

9. Arrange the blocks and sew together as shown in Fig. 5. The top block is pointed down, 5 blocks are pointed up, 6 blocks are pointed down and the bottom block is pointed up.

10. **Block 3**. Sew using the following pieces:
- 16 each - $2^3/8$" small red print and yellow HST's
- 48 yellow and 16 small red print $4^1/4$" QST's
- 64 green, 32 blue print and 8 red print $2^5/8$" squares.

11. See the Fig. 6 for the arrangement of pieces. Sew pieces together in diagonal columns, then sew the columns together. Make 8 blocks. Sew 4 blocks together (see Fig. 7, Section B). Make 2 rows.

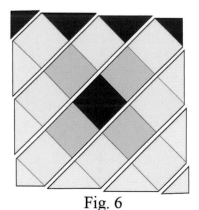

Fig. 6

12. Sew Fig. 7 below for arranging sections for sewing. Sew a 38" stripe piece to the top and bottom of section A. Sew a section B to the top and bottom edges.

13. Sew a 62" blue tonal piece to each side edge. Sew section C to the right edge.

14. Sew a 61" green border piece to each side edge. Sew a 55" green border piece to the top and bottom edges.

Fig. 7

15. Sew a 64" red print border piece to each side edge. Sew a 60" red border piece to the top and bottom edges.

Completing the quilt:

Follow the quilting instructions on page 62 to layer and quilt as desired. Our quilt was machine long arm quilted.

Follow the binding instructions on page 63 to attach the binding.

FINISHED QUILT SIZE - 52" x 68" (145 cm x 173 cm)
FINISHED BLOCK SIZE -
    Small blocks 8" x 8" (20 cm x 20 cm),
    Large blocks 16" x 16" (41 cm x 41 cm)

Fabric requirements:

The yardage requirement is based on 43" to 44" (109/112 cm) wide fabric

- $1^1/_2$ yds (1.37 m) - turquoise large floral print fabric
- 1 yd (91 cm) - lavender print fabric
- $^3/_4$ yd (69 cm) - turquoise small geometric print fabric
- $^1/_8$ yd (12 cm) - light turquoise small floral print fabric
- $1^1/_4$ yds (1.14 m) - yellow small floral print fabric
- $^1/_2$ yd (46 cm) - turquoise tonal fabric
- $^5/_8$ yd (57 cm) - blue tonal fabric
- $^1/_2$ yd (46 cm) - dark wine small geometric print fabric
- $^1/_2$ yd (46 cm) - fabric for binding
- $3^1/_2$ yds (3.20 m) - fabric for backing

You will also need:
60" x 76" (152 cm x 193 cm) piece of batting
Coordinating thread for quilting

Garden Maze

Cutting the pieces:

Follow Rotary Cutting instructions on page 61 to cut the fabric. Cut pieces from selvage to selvage. The measurements include ¼" seam allowance. The borders are cut longer than necessary. Trim after sewing.

Note - if you are using fabric with the design one direction for the half square triangles, cut half of the triangles diagonally one direction and the half the opposite direction.

From the turquoise large floral print fabric:
Cut 4 blocks 8½" square.
Cut 14 blocks 8⅞" square. Cut the blocks diagonally for 28 half square triangles (HST's).

From the lavender floral print fabric:
Cut 3 blocks 8⅞" square. Cut the block diagonally for 6 HST's.
Cut 2 pieces 3⅛" x 16½".
Cut 2 pieces 3⅜" x 12½". Cut each end at a 45° degree angle as shown below.

From the turquoise small geometric print fabric:
Cut 2 pieces 3⅛" x 16½".
Cut 2 blocks 8⅞" square. Cut the block diagonally for 4 HST's.

From the turquoise small floral print fabric:
Cut 2 pieces 3⅜" x 18⅛". Cut each end at a 45° angle.

From the yellow floral print:
Cut 2 pieces 6⅛" x 23⅞". Cut each end at a 45° angle.
Cut 12 blocks 8⅞" square. Cut the block diagonally for 24 HST's.

From the turquoise tonal print fabric:
Cut 2 blocks 8⅞" square. Cut the block diagonally for 4 HST's.
Cut 2 pieces 3⅛" x 16½".
Cut 1 block 4⅞" square. Cut the block diagonally for 2 HST's.

From the blue tonal fabric:
Cut 2 pieces 3⅜" x 23⅞". Cut each end at a 45° angle. Cut a right side border piece 2½" x 72" (Cut and piece for 72").
Cut a top border piece 2½" x 56" (Cut and piece for 56").

From the wine small geometric print fabric:
Cut a right side border piece 2½" x 72" (Cut and piece for 72").
Cut a bottom border piece 2½" x 56" (Cut and piece for 56").

For the binding:
Cut 6½ strips 2½" x width of fabric.

Assembling the quilt top:

Sew all pieces right sides together and sew with a ¼" seam allowance. Press all seams as you sew, pressing the seams toward the darker fabric.

1. **Block 1.** Sew two 8⅞" HST's together in the following combinations to make the number of blocks shown (Fig. 1):

- 18 blocks - turquoise large floral print and yellow floral print
- 2 blocks - turquoise large floral print and turquoise tonal print
- 4 blocks - turquoise large floral print and turquoise small geometric print
- 2 blocks - turquoise large floral print and lavender floral print
- 2 blocks - yellow floral print and turquoise tonal print
- 4 blocks - yellow floral print and lavender floral print

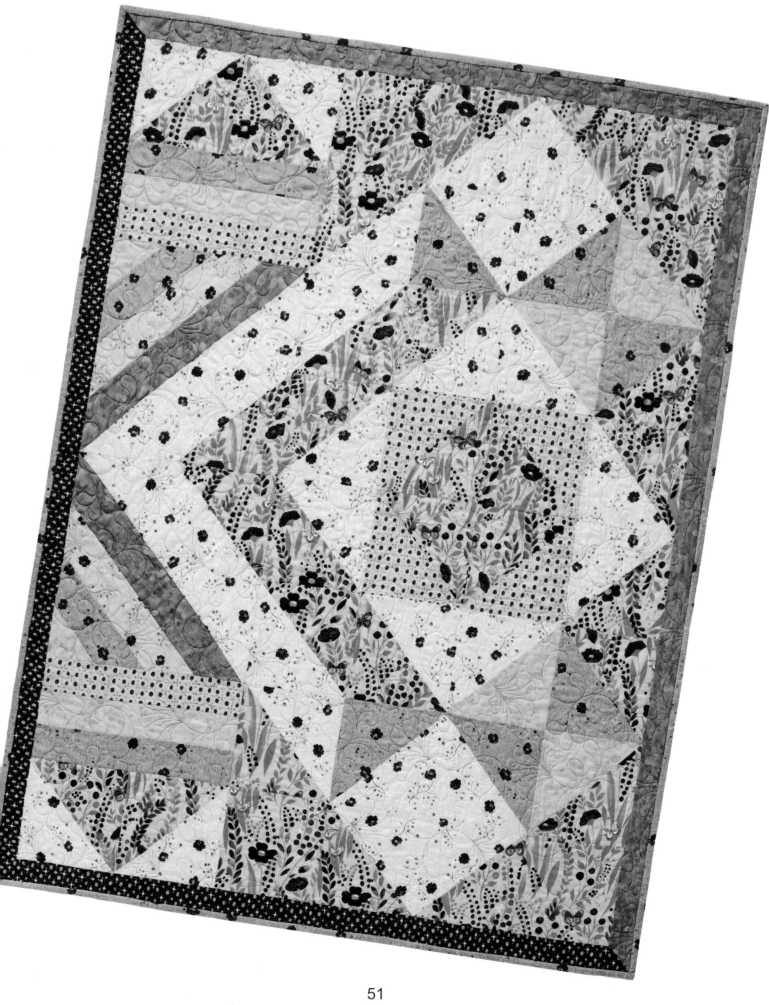

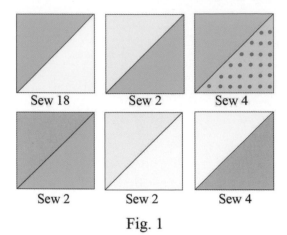

Sew 18   Sew 2   Sew 4

Sew 2   Sew 2   Sew 4

Fig. 1

2. **Block 2**. Sew the 16$\frac{1}{2}$" pieces together in the following order: lavender floral, turquoise tonal, and turquoise geometric. See Fig. 2. Make 2 units.

3. Sew 2 turquoise large print/yellow print HST blocks together, sewing on the turquoise edges (Fig. 2). Make 2. Sew the HST two-block row to the 16$\frac{1}{2}$" strip unit, sewing to the lavender piece. Make 2 blocks.

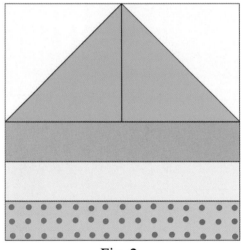

Fig. 2

4. **Block 3**. See Fig. 3 for arrangement of the pieces. Sew the block in 2 sections.

• Sew a turquoise large floral print HST to the short edge of the 23$\frac{7}{8}$" yellow floral piece. Make 2.
• Sew the blue tonal piece, the turquoise small floral print piece, the lavender floral piece and the turquoise tonal HST together. Make 2.
• Sew the 2 sections together, sewing the yellow floral edge to the blue tonal edge. Make 2 blocks.

Fig. 3

5. See Fig. 4, section A for the layout for the quilt. Sew a Block 2 and Block 3 together. Make 2. Sew these 2 two-block units together.

6. See the row arrangement for the HST blocks in Fig. 4, section B. Sew an 8$\frac{1}{8}$" square turquoise large print block on each side of 2 HST's blocks on the top and bottom rows. Sew the HST blocks together with 4 in each row, arranged as shown. Sew the rows together.

7. Sew section A to the left edge of the section B.

Follow the instructions on page 62 for mitering the border corners. Sew the blue tonal border pieces to the top and right side edges. Sew the wine small geometric print border pieces to the bottom and left side edges.

Completing the quilt:

Follow the quilting instructions on page 62 to layer and quilt as desired. Our quilt was machine long arm quilted.

Follow the binding instructions on page 63 to attach the binding.

Fig. 4

FINISHED QUILT BLOCK SIZE - 50³/₄" x 50³/₄" (129 cm x 129 cm)
FINISHED BLOCK SIZE - 9³/₈" x 9³/₈" (24 cm x 24 cm)

Fabric requirements:

The yardage requirement is based on 43" to 44" (109/112 cm) wide fabric.

- 1 yd (91 cm) - yellow print fabric
- ³/₄ yd (69 cm) - orange tonal fabric
- 1¹/₄ yds (1.14 m) - blue tonal fabric
- ³/₈ yd (34 cm) - green bird print fabric
- ³/₈ yd (34 cm) - blue floral fabric
- ³/₈ yd (34 cm) - sage green tonal fabric
- ¹/₄ yd (23 cm) - bright green tonal fabric
- ⁵/₈ yd (57 cm) - light bright green tonal fabric
- ¹/₄ yd (23 cm) - pale sage green tonal fabric
- ¹/₂ yd (46 cm) - fabric for binding
- 3¹/₂ yds (3.20 m) - fabric for backing

You will also need:
59" x 59" (150 cm x 150 cm) piece of batting
Fusible web with paper backing
Coordinating thread for quilting and appliqué

Cutting the pieces:

Follow Rotary Cutting instructions on page 61 to cut the fabric. Cut pieces from selvage to selvage. The measurements include ¹/₄" seam allowance. The borders and long strip pieces are cut longer than necessary. Trim after sewing.

See page 62 for instructions on cutting the fusible web appliqué pieces.

From the yellow print fabric:
Cut 48 pieces 3¹/₄" square. Cut diagonally for 96 half square triangles (HST's).
Cut 9 flowers for appliqué using the pattern on page 59.
Cut 4 flower centers for appliqué using the pattern on page 59.

From the orange tonal fabric:
Cut 1 piece 1¹/₂" x 42".
Cut 1 piece 1¹/₂" x 41".
Cut 3¹/₂ strips 1³/₄" x width of fabric (150" total).
Cut 4 flowers for appliqué using the pattern on page 59.
Cut 9 flower centers for appliqué using the pattern on page 59.

Cutting continued on page 56

A Splash of Flowers

From the blue tonal fabric:
Cut 1 piece 4" x 53" (Cut and piece to get 53").
Cut 1 piece 4" x 51" (Cut and piece to get 51").
Cut 1 piece 4" x 45" (Cut and piece to get 45").
Cut 1 piece 4" x 42".
Cut 16 pieces $3^1/4$" square. Cut diagonally for 32 HST's.

From the green bird print fabric:
Cut $3^1/2$ strips $1^3/4$" x width of fabric (150" total).
Cut 4 pieces $5^3/4$" square.

From the blue floral print fabric:
Cut $3^1/2$ strips $1^3/4$" x width of fabric (150" total).
Cut 16 pieces $2^7/8$" square.

From the sage green tonal fabric:
Cut $3^1/2$ strips $1^3/4$" x width of fabric (150" total).
Cut 1 piece $7^1/8$" square.
Cut 3 pieces $5^3/4$" square.

From the bright green tonal fabric:
Cut 1 piece $7^1/8$" square.
Cut 3 pieces $5^3/4$" square.

From the light bright green tonal fabric:
Cut 48 pieces $3^1/4$" square. Cut diagonally for 96 HST's.
Cut 1 piece $7^1/8$" square.
Cut 4 pieces $5^3/4$" square.

From the pale sage green tonal fabric:
Cut 1 piece $7^1/8$" square.
Cut 3 pieces $5^3/4$" square.

For the binding:
Cut 5 strips $2^1/2$" x width of fabric.

Assembling the quilt top:

*Sew all pieces right sides together and sew with a $1/4$"
seam allowance. Press all seams as you sew, pressing
the seams toward the darker fabric.*

1. **Block 1**. Sew a $3^1/4$" blue tonal HST to 2
   edges of the $2^7/8$" square blue floral piece. See
   Fig. 1 for arrangement of pieces. Make 16.

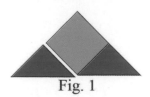

Fig. 1

2. Sew a unit made in number 1 above to 2
   opposite edges of a $7^1/8$" green square piece.
   Sew a unit to the remaining 2 edges. Make 4
   blocks using the 4 assorted $7^1/8$" green pieces.

Fig. 2

3. **Block 2.** Sew a $3^1/4$" light bright green HST to
   a $3^1/4$" yellow HST. Make 96. Using 48 of the
   blocks, sew 2 HST blocks together arranged
   as shown in the Fig. 3, B. Make 24. Sew 2
   rows together. Make 12 blocks (Fig. 3, C).

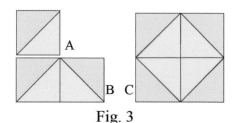

Fig. 3

4. In this order, sew the $1^3/4$" orange, green
   bird print, blue floral print and sage green
   wide strips together. Cutting across the
   strips, cut 48 pieces $2^7/8$" long (Fig. 4).

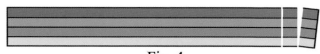

Fig. 4

5. Sew a $2^7/8$" strip unit to 2 opposite edges of
   a HST block unit (see Fig. 5). Sew the strip
   units so that the fabric arrangement is the
   opposite direction on each edge. Make 12.

Fig. 5

6. Sew a HST block unit to each end of the remaining 24 strip units. See Fig. 6 for arrangement of the HST blocks and strips and the direction to turn the HST blocks. Sew a HST/strip block unit to each side edge (Fig. 6).

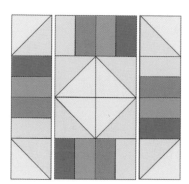

Fig. 6

7. Sew 4 blocks to make a row. Sew 2 rows with Block 1, the blue blocks, as shown in Fig. 7. Sew these 2 rows together.

8. See the appliqué instructions on page 62. Fuse and appliqué the yellow flower centers to the 4 orange flowers. See the arrangement for the appliqué flowers in Fig. 9 and fuse the flowers to the blue blocks, fusing the flowers slightly off center of each block. Appliqué the flowers.

Fig. 7

9. Sew 4 Block 2's together to make 2 rows. See Fig. 8. Sew these 2 rows together and sew to the 2 rows completed in number 8 above.

10. Sew the 41" orange piece to the left edge of the block unit. Sew the 42" orange piece to the top edge. Trim ends (Fig. 8).

11. Sew the 42" blue piece to the left edge. Sew the 45" blue piece to the top edge (Fig. 8).

12. Sew 9 of the $5\frac{3}{4}$" green square blocks together in a random color arrangement. Sew the remaining 8 blocks together. Sew the 8 block unit to the left edge, then sew the 9 block unit to the top edge. (Fig. 8).

13. Sew the 51" blue piece to the left edge, then sew the 53" blue piece to the top edge.

Fig. 8

14. Fuse and appliqué the orange flower centers to the yellow flowers. Arrange the yellow flowers on the green blocks and blue borders as shown in Fig. 9. Alternate the flowers from side to side. Fuse and appliqué.

Fig. 9

Completing the quilt:

Follow the quilting instructions on page 62 to layer and quilt as desired. Our quilt was machine quilted in a meandering pattern.

Follow the binding instructions on page 63 to attach the binding.

Splash of Flowers - Appliqué pattern

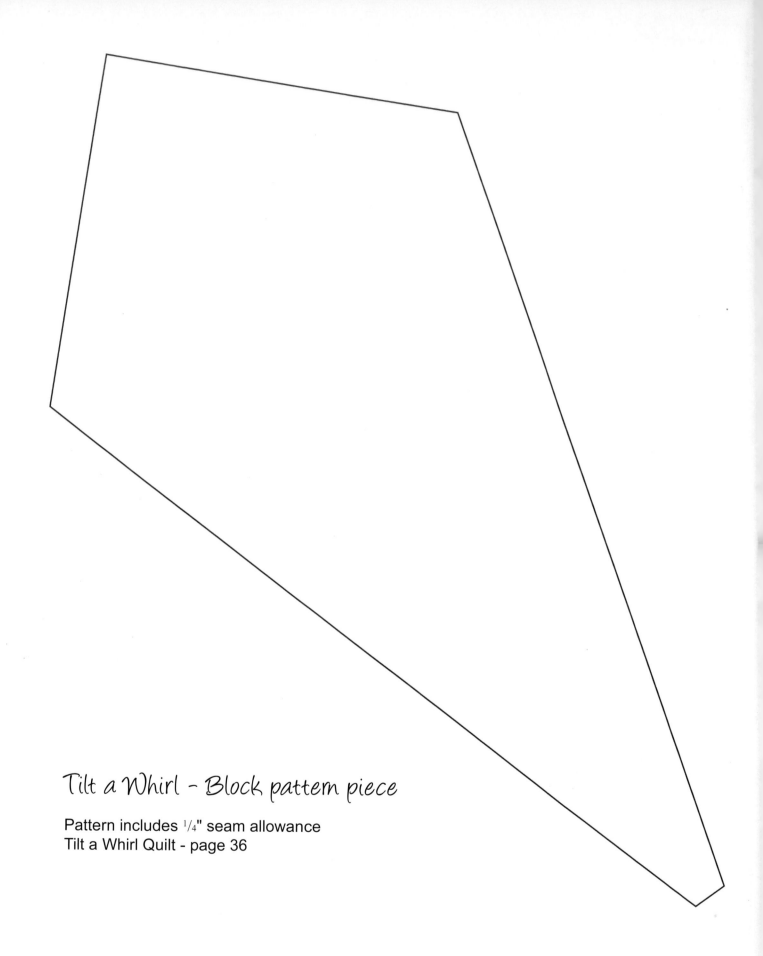

Tilt a Whirl - Block pattern piece

Pattern includes $1/4$" seam allowance
Tilt a Whirl Quilt - page 36

General Instructions

Fabrics:

Choose high quality medium weight 100% cotton fabrics. Cotton fabrics are easier to quilt with than blended fabrics. The yardage requirements are based on 43"/44" fabrics and allow for trimming the selvages and should provide ample fabric.

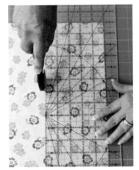 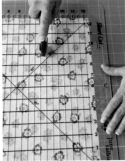

Fig. 1   *Fig. 2*

Rotary Cutting:

Rotary cutting provides speed and accuracy to your cutting. Cut strips and sub-cut into pieces. Easy triangles are cut by cutting the strips into squares, then cutting the squares diagonally for Half Square Triangles (HST's). Squares can be cut in half diagonally twice for Quarter Square Triangles (QST's).

Fold fabric in half lengthwise, right sides out. Trim selves and square bottom edges to selvage. Cut strips across the width of the fabric, selvage to selvage. Cut the strips the size required, aligning the ruler markings to the correct size and cut (Fig. 1).

For cutting multiple strips, use a ruler with multiple slots to cut several strips with one placement of the ruler (Fig. 2). Rulers are available for various increments of sizes for strip cutting.

Machine Piecing:

1. Sew with a sewing machine stitch length of 11 stitches per inch.
2. Use a general or all purpose thread for the needle and bobbin.
3. Sew with an exact $1/4$" seam. This is very important for accurate piecing.
4. Sew with pieces right sides together, matching raw edges. Pin all pieces prior to sewing to prevent fabrics from slipping during stitching.
5. Trim points that extend beyond the sewn edges.
6. At the intersection of seams, press the seams in opposite directions to prevent fabric thickness.

Pressing:

Press after sewing each seam with a steam iron set on cotton setting. Turn the seams in one direction, toward the darker fabric and press. Occasionally, you may need to press seams open flat to prevent bulk.

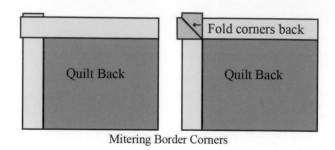
Mitering Border Corners

Fusible Web Appliqué:

Follow the instructions provide by the manufacture for use of the fusible web.

If you are using a light color fabric for the appliqué, you may need to line the fabric with fusible interfacing prior to attaching the fusible web. This will prevent the darker fabrics from showing through.

Photocopy the patterns. **Permission is granted to photocopy the patterns for personal use in making the quilts in this book.**

1. Place the fusible web with the fabric side up. Cut the appliqué pattern out and place it upside down on the paper side of the fusible web. Trace around the pattern. Repeat for as many pieces as needed.
2. Trim the paper backing/fusible web ¼" around the outside of the appliqué design. Do not remove the paper.
3. Place the appliqué cut-out on the wrong side of the fabric with the paper side up. Fuse according to the manufacturer's settings and instructions.
4. With sharp scissors, cut the appliqué along the pattern lines. Remove paper backing.
5. Arrange the appliqué piece on the quilt top with the web side down. Fuse.
6. Appliqué edges with a narrow zig zag satin stitch.

Mitering the Borders:

Center a border piece on each edge of the quilt, right sides together and pin. Each border piece will have a loose end on each edge that is more than equal the width of the border. Sew each border, starting and stopping ¼" from each edge of the quilt.

With the quilt wrong side up, fold 1 border piece back at a 45° angle, aligning to the point that the sewing stopped at ¼". Use a ruler with a 45° angle shown to verify fold and press. Repeat with the adjacent border piece. Align the fold creases, right sides together and sew. After you have verified that the corner border section is flat, with no gaps, trim the seam. Repeat for each corner.

Quilt Backing:

The yardage requirements provided for the quilt backing is based on 43"/44" wide fabric. To allow for possible shifting when quilting, the backing should be 4" larger than the quilt top on all sides.

1. To piece the backing, add 8" to the length and width of the quilt top. Cut 2 length of fabrics to the length measurement including the 8".
2. Trim selvages. Place the 2 lengths of fabrics right sides together. Sew together on both long edges to form a tube. Press seams open.
3. Fold fabrics lengthwise, centering the seams to match (Fig. 3). Press one side folded edge. Cut on the pressed fold and open flat (Fig. 4).

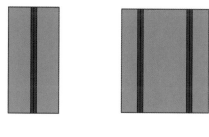

Fig. 3   **Fig. 4**

Batting:

Choose the batting based on the desired result of your quilt. A cotton or cotton blend batting is easy to work with, grips the fabric, gives a low loft, and is easy to machine quilt. If you want a fluffy or thick quilt, choose a high loft or extra loft batting.

Cut your batting the same size as the backing, adding 8" to quilt top width and height.

Assembling the Quilt:

1. On the back side of the quilt, trim any seams as needed and cut all loose threads. Press the quilt top.

2. Lay the quilt backing **wrong** side up on a flat surface. Use masking tape to tape the edges to the surface, pulling the fabric smooth. Lay the batting on the backing and smooth the batting without stretching. Lay the quilt top **right** side up centered on the batting.

3. Using quilter's safety pins, pin through all layers starting in the center and working out. Space the pins approximately 4" apart. If the pins are in the quilting paths, remove while quilting.

Quilting:

Use a general purpose thread in the quilt bobbin. For the top thread, use a general purpose thread or a variegated thread to blend with the fabrics. To make the quilting lines show more, use a contrasting color or other threads such as a metallic thread.

Follow the instructions for your sewing machine for quilting. Some sewing machines have special attachments or pressure feet for quilting. Use a stitch length of 6 to 10 stitches per inch. Begin quilting in the center and quilt outward. Lock the stitches at the beginning and end of each quilting line.

Types of quilting:

- *In the Ditch* - quilting along the seams or appliqué pieces.
- *Outline Quilting* - quilting a distance, usually $1/4$" from the seams or appliqué pieces.
- *Echo Quilting* - quilting around an appliqué piece or pieced design with two or more parallel lines.
- *Free motion quilting* - quilting in a random pattern. Use a darning foot for this quilting and lower your feed dog. Place one hand on the quilt on each side of the darning foot on the quilt to smoothly move the fabric while stitching. Move the quilt back and forth, sideways or in a circular motion to create a free form meandering design. Use a steady machine speed.

Binding:

Trim excess batting and backing fabric even with the quilt top edges. Trim to square up the corners and sides to make as straight and even as possible.

1. Sew the binding strips right sides together diagonally end to end to form 1 long continuous strip (Fig. 5).

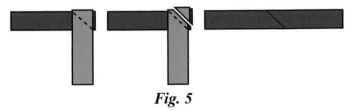

Fig. 5

2. Fold the strip in half lengthwise, wrong sides together and press.

3. Starting at the center of the bottom edge of the top side of the quilt, place the binding on the edge of the quilt, aligning the raw edges of the binding to the quilt. Start sewing 6" from the end of the binding, using a $1/4$" seam allowance to sew through all layers (Fig. 6).

Fig. 6

4. Stop sewing $1/4$" from a corner (Fig. 7). Cut threads.

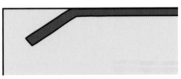

Fig. 7

5. Fold the binding up at a 45 degree angle (Fig. 8).

Fig. 8

6. Holding the fold in place, fold the binding down with the fold aligned with the raw edges. Pin. Start sewing at the edge of the quilt, sewing through all layers (Fig. 9).

Fig.9

7. Continue sewing the binding to the quilt, stopping 6" from the starting point. Unfold the beginning and

ending tails of the binding and place beginning end of the binding over the ending tail. Draw a diagonal line on the ending tail even with the diagonal end of the beginning tail. Cut the tail end ¹/₂" longer than the diagonal line. Pin ends together and sew. Press seam and refold the binding. Press edge. Finish sewing the binding to the top side of the quilt.

8. Fold the binding over the quilt edge to the back of the quilt and pin the pressed edge. Be sure to cover any machine stitching (Fig. 10).

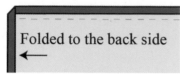

Fig. 10

Fold the binding over an adjacent quilt edge to miter the corners and pin (Fig. 11).

Fig. 11

9. Hand sew the binding to the back of the quilt with a blind stitch (Fig. 12).

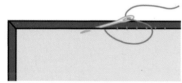

Fig. 12

Labeling your quilt:

Your quilt will be an heirloom for future generations! You should label your quilt to provide as much information as possible about yourself and the quilt.

On a plain piece of fabric, use a permanent marker to write information such as the name of the quilt, your name, your location or address, the date and any other information you wish to add. Hand sew or appliqué the label to the back of your quilt.

Sources:

Many thanks to these companies for furnishing products for use in this book.

Quilting Treasures (QuiltingTreasures.com) - Fabric collections used in the quilts on the following pages:
Pg. 4 - *Groove On*
Pg. 22 - *Country Goodness*
Pg. 28 - *Laila*
Pg. 36 - *Splendid Rhapsody*
Pg. 42 - *Friends*
Pg. 54 - *Birds of a Feather*

Clothworks (Clothworkstextiles.com) - Fabric collections used in the quilts on the following pages:
Pg. 16 - *Hydrangeas*
Pg. 48 - *Paintbrush Gardens*

Henry Glass (Henryglassfabrics.com) - Fabric collection used in the quilt on the following page:
Pg. 10 - *Colour Vie*

The Warm Company (warmcompany.com) - Warm & Natural® cotton batting, Seam a Steam 2® fusible web.

Sulky (Sulky.com) - Rayon thread and Blendables thread.

June Tailor (Junetailor.com) - Assorted sizes of slotted strip rulers for rotary strip cutting.

Olfa (Olfa.com) - Frosted non-slip ruler for rotary cutting, rotary cutter, and cutting mat.

And a special thanks also to:

Becky Stayner (Sunnyhousestudio.com) for beautiful photography. All of the quilts were photographed in her wonderful and amazing studio.

Lisa Mullins (Wanderingstitches.com) for beautiful machine quilting on all the quilts except *A Splash of Flowers*.

My husband Danny, for his patience and support while I was working on this book.